Chimps Use Tools!

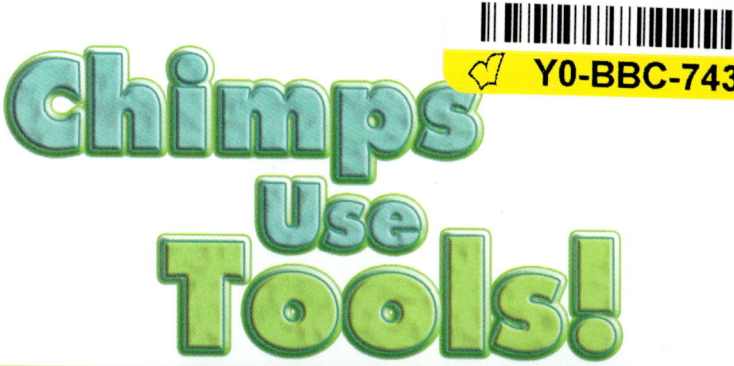

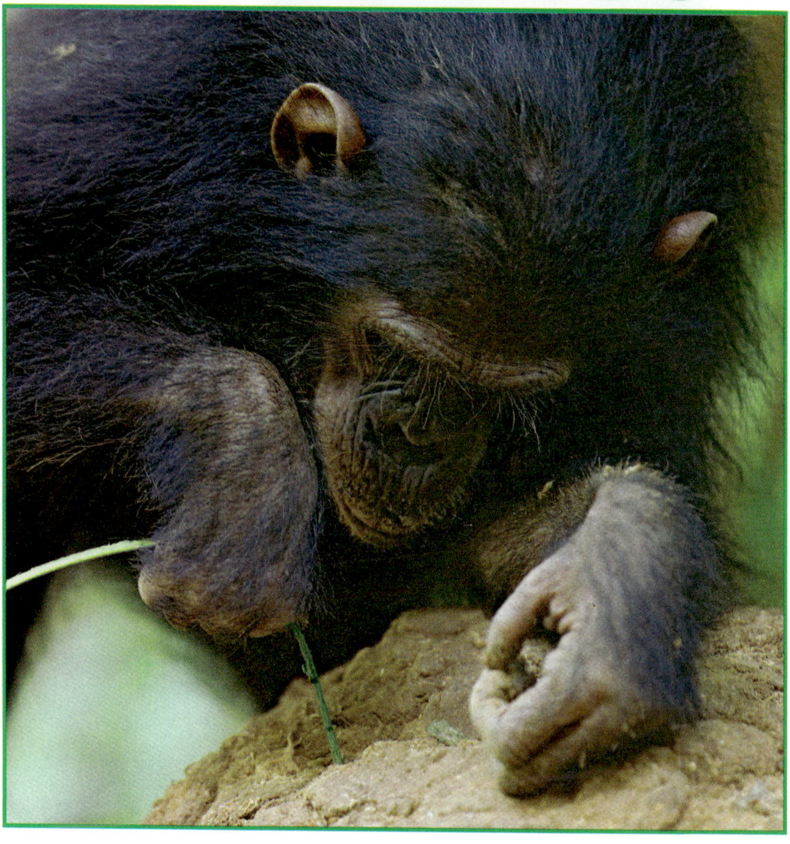

by Paul Bernard

PEARSON

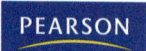

Glenview, Illinois • Boston, Massachusetts • Chandler, Arizona
Upper Saddle River, New Jersey

chimpanzee (chimp)

mound

Chimps like to eat termites.
But termites are not easy to catch.
They build big strong mounds to live in.
The termites are safe in their mounds.

There are holes in the termite mound.
Termites can go in.
Termites can go out.
The chimp's fingers are too big for the holes.
The termites are safe for now.

The termites are deep inside the mound.
The chimp cannot reach them.
How will the chimp get them out?
Chimps can use tools to catch the termites!

The chimp finds a good tool.

First, the chimp finds a good tool.
The tool must be long and thin.
The tool can be a piece of grass.
The tool can be a stick.

The chimp uses the tool.

The chimp puts the stick into a hole.
The termites in the mound now see the stick.
They cannot see the chimp above.

The termites bite the stick.

The chimp holds the stick in the hole.
The termites bite the stick.
They hold on to the stick.
The termites are about to be caught.

The chimp eats the termites.

Finally, the chimp pulls out the stick.
There are termites on the stick.
The chimp eats the termites.
The chimp puts the stick into another hole.
The chimp will eat many termites today!